Time, Money, Measurement

Projects and Activities Across the Curriculum

Written by Denise Bieniek

Illustrated by Laura Ferraro

10 9 8 7 6 5 4 3

This edition published in 2003.

Troll Early Learning Activities

W9-BHJ-061

Troll Early Learning Activities is a classroom-tested series designed to provide time-pressured teachers with a wide range of theme-related projects and activities to enhance lesson plans and enrich the curriculum. Each book focuses on a different area of early childhood learning, from math and writing to art and science. Using a wide range of activities, each title in this series is chockful of innovative ideas, handy reproducible pages, puzzles and games, classroom projects, suggestions for bulletin boards and learning centers, and much more.

With highly interactive student projects and teacher suggestions that make learning fun, Troll Early Learning Activities is an invaluable classroom resource you'll turn to again and again. We hope you will enjoy using the worksheets and activities presented in these books. And we know your students will benefit from the dynamic, creative learning environment you have created!

Titles in this series:

Animal Friends: Projects and Activities for Grades K-3

Circle Time Fun: Projects and Activities for Grades Pre-K-2

Classroom Decorations: Ideas for a Creative Classroom

Early Literacy Skills: Projects and Activities for Grades K-3

Helping Hands: Small Motor Skills Projects and Activities

Hi, Neighbor! Projects and Activities About Our Community

Number Skills: Math Projects and Activities for Grades K-3

People of the World: Multicultural Projects and Activities

Our World: Science Projects and Activities for Grades K-3

Seasons and Holidays: Celebrations All Year Long

Story Time: Skill-Building Projects and Activities for Grades K-3

Time, Money, Measurement: Projects and Activities Across the Curriculum

---

Metric Conversion Chart

1 inch = 2.54 cm	1 foot = .305 m	1 yard = .914 m
1 mile = 1.61 km	1 fluid ounce = 29.573 ml	1 cup = .24 l
1 pint = .473 l	1 teaspoon = 4.93 ml	1 tablespoon = 14.78 ml

Contents

Rhyming Clocks 5–6

What Time Is It? 7–8

Time Teasers 9

Time to Match 10

How Long! Worksheet 11

The Magician's Hat 12–14

Night and Day Interactive Poster 15–17

The Order of Things Game 18–19

Piggy Bank Bulletin Board 20–21

Golfing for "Dollars" 22

Money Worksheet 23

Dee's Discount Shop......................................24

Money Wheel..25

Pass the Buck..26–27

Famous Faces..28

Nursery Measurements 29

Sorting Trees Bulletin Board 30–31

Nonstandard Estimations 32

Oh, What a Tangled Web!................................33

Party Time! 34

Treasure Hunt 35

Telephone Match 36–37

Sports Day 38–39

Fraction Bingo 40–43

Missing Fractions...44

Fun with Fractions 45

Roman Numerals 46

Roman Holiday..47

Counting in Roman Numerals 48

Farm Chores File-Folder Game 49–52

Sarah's Secret Plan 53–55

Time Charts...56

Sarah's Story 57

Sarah's Schedule 58

My Weekly Schedule 59

Timed Test 60–61

Time Award 62

Math Award 63

Answers 64

Rhyming Clocks

- crayons or markers
- scissors
- oaktag
- glue
- hole puncher
- brass fasteners

Glue

Directions:

1. Reproduce the clock art on page 6 for each student. Ask students to color the clocks and hands, mount them on oaktag, and cut them out.

2. Show students how to use a hole puncher to make holes in the ends of he hands. Then show students how to use scissors to make a hole in the center of the face of the clock.

3. Have students lay the two hands on the clock face, holes overlapping with one another. Stick a brass fastener through all three layers and open the ends in back so that the hands are securely fastened to the clock.

4. Repeat the following rhyme for the class, encouraging those who know it to join in:

> Hickory, dickory, dock
> The mouse ran up the clock.
> The clock struck one,
> And down he ran.
> Hickory, dickory, dock.

5. Ask the class what time was mentioned in the rhyme. Have them set their clocks to 1:00 and repeat the rhyme.

6. Then ask the class to think of new rhymes for 2:00 through 12:00. Remind them to rhyme a word with the number showing on their clocks. For example:

> Hickory, dickory, dock
> The mouse ran up the clock.
> The clock struck two,
> The mouse lost his shoe.
> Hickory, dickory, dock.

7. As volunteers create new rhymes, have them repeat them for their classmates. Then ask the children to move the hands on their clocks to match the time in the new rhyme.

8. You may also wish to ask students to write their rhymes on paper with a clock glued to each sheet. These can be stored in a folder for students' use during free time. When students wish to play with them, they can recite the verse and then move the hands to match the time. Clocks showing the correct time may be glued to the back of each sheet of paper so that students may self-check.

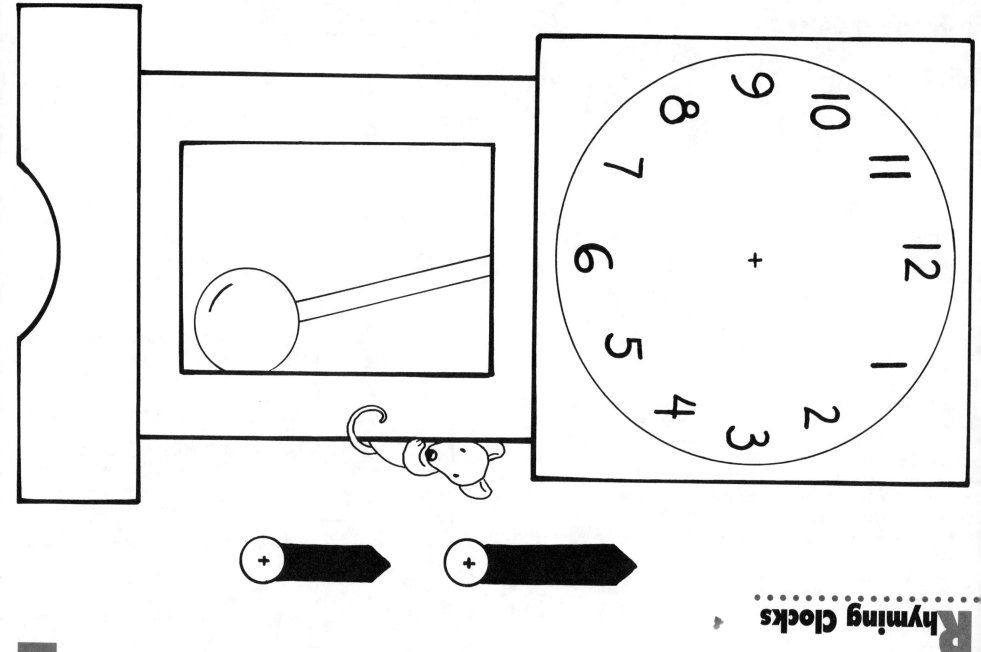

Rhyming Clocks

What Time Is It?

Materials:

* crayons or markers
* scissors
* oaktag
* rubber cement
* plastic bags or paper lunch bags

Directions:

1. Reproduce the clock puzzle art on page 8 once for each student. Ask students to color their clocks.

2. Demonstrate how to brush rubber cement onto the back of the clock and onto a piece of oaktag that is sized just slightly larger than the clock. While the rubber cement is still tacky, show the class how to fold each clock in half, glued sides out.

3. Have students lay one edge of their clocks onto the oaktag, and then slowly unfold the clocks, smoothing them onto the oaktag as they go.

4. Direct students' attention to the dotted lines on their clocks. Inform them that these are the lines of the puzzle pieces. Demonstrate how to cut along these lines to separate the pieces.

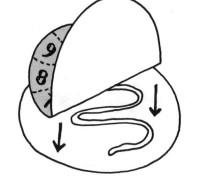

5. When all the pieces have been cut, allow plenty of time for students to put their puzzles back together. Tell students having a hard time with their puzzles to look at the classroom clock. Point out that the numbers on a clock go in order around the face of the clock. When it is time to put the puzzles away, hand out plastic bags or paper lunch bags and have students store their puzzle in the bags.

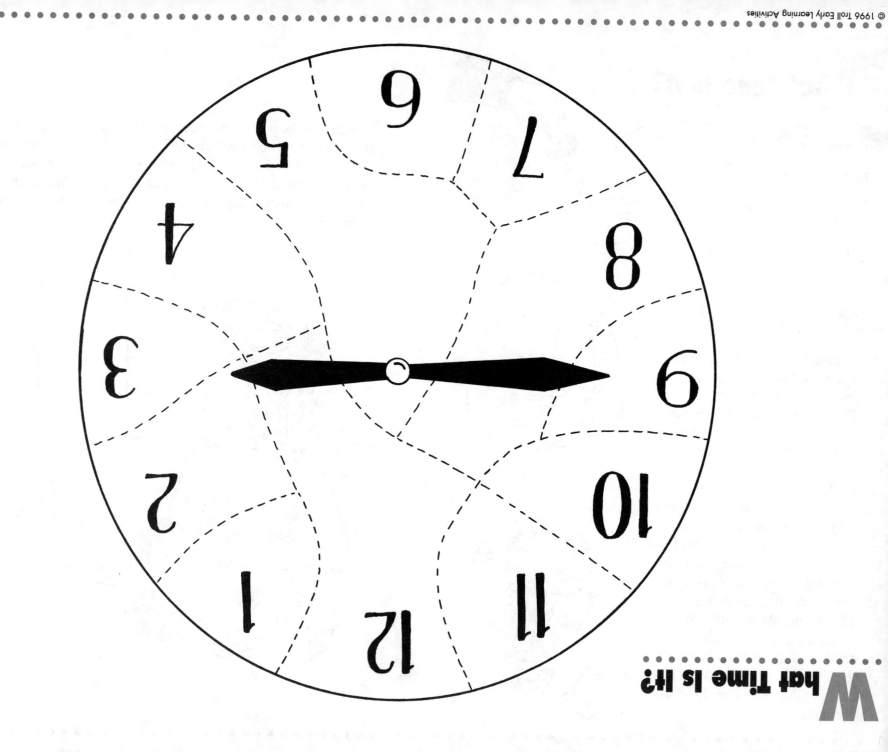

What Time Is It?

Time Teasers

Figure out the answers to the questions below. Show your work.

1. Clem claimed he ran a mile in 2 minutes and 32 seconds. Dave said, "That's nothing. I once ran a mile in only 152 seconds!" Who was really the fastest? _____

2. Tracey and Claudia were at the ice skating rink. Tracey said that she could do 10 laps in 3 minutes. Claudia replied that she could do 20 laps in 5 minutes. Who can do more laps per minute? _____

3. Doug told his friends that he once climbed a mountain in 180 minutes. How many hours did it take Doug to climb the mountain?

4. One mother said her baby got his first tooth when he was just 30 weeks old. Another mother said her baby got his first tooth when he was 6 months old. Which baby got his first tooth at a younger age?

5. Grandpa was born in 1928, and he loved to talk about the great flood of 1943. How old was Grandpa at the time of the flood?

Time to Match

Materials:

- oaktag
- scissors
- permanent markers
- hole puncher
- different-colored yarn
- plastic hanger
- paper clips

Directions:

1. Cut pieces of oaktag into ten 6" squares or some other similarly sized shape. On five of the squares, write a time digitally. On the remaining five squares, draw clock faces and show the same times again.

2. In the top center and bottom center of each square, punch a hole, about 1" in from the edge. Tie a 6" length of yarn to the top hole in each square.

3. Place the squares in pairs, matching times shown digitally and on a clock face. Tie five squares, one from each of the pairs, to the bottom edge of a hanger.

4. Unfold five paper clips into an S shape. Tie the free end of the lengths of yarn on the remaining five squares to a paper clip each.

5. To use the activity, demonstrate to the class how to match the times. Hold up one square and ask someone to read the time it shows. Then hand the square to the reader and ask him or her to hook it into the hole of the matching square that is hanging off the hanger.

6. Other hangers may be made and hung about the room for students' use during free time. Vary the game by writing out times in words (for example, "ten thirty") and having students match those with digital and clock times.

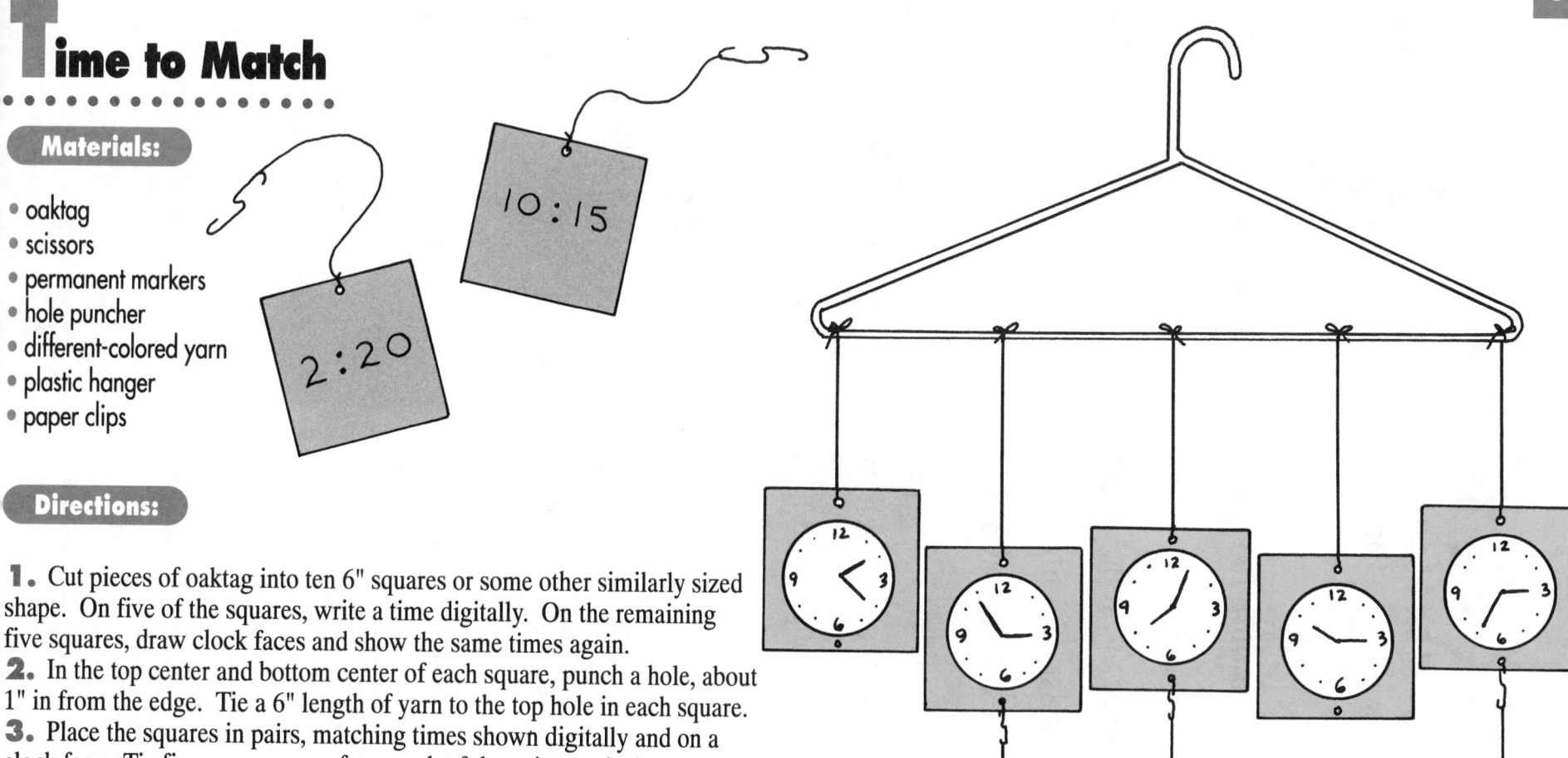

How Long! Worksheet

Pair up with a classmate. You will need a watch or a clock with a second hand. Perform the following tasks while your partner times you. Then switch roles.

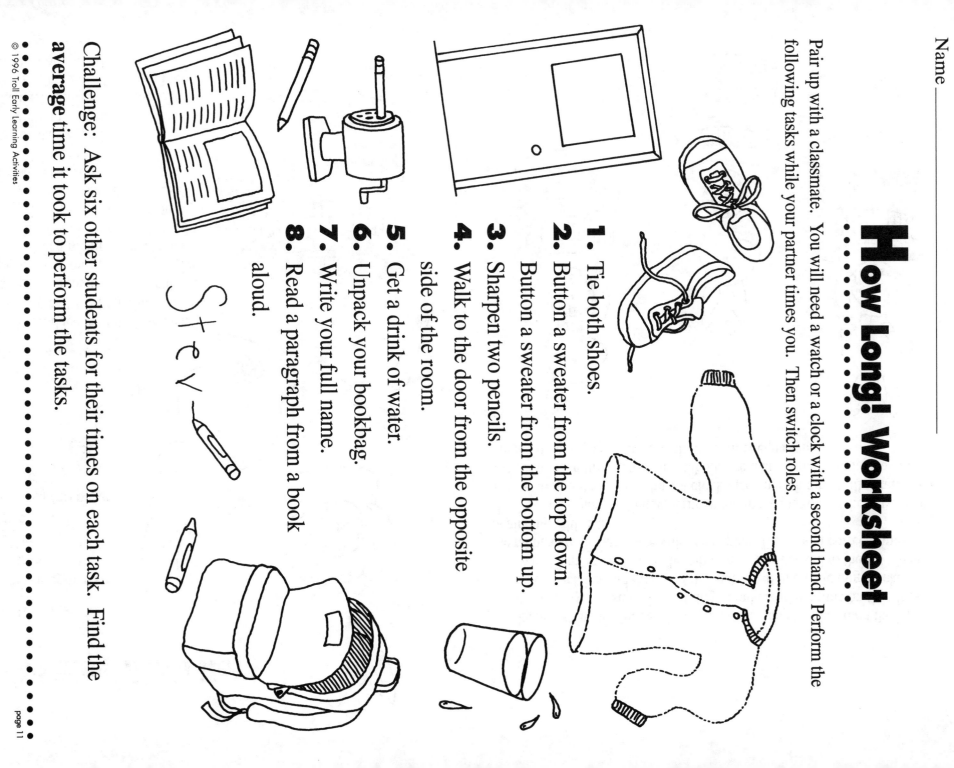

1. Tie both shoes.

2. Button a sweater from the top down. Button a sweater from the bottom up.

3. Sharpen two pencils.

4. Walk to the door from the opposite side of the room.

5. Get a drink of water.

6. Unpack your bookbag.

7. Write your full name.

8. Read a paragraph from a book aloud.

Stev

Challenge: Ask six other students for their times on each task. Find the **average** time it took to perform the tasks.

The Magician's Hat

Materials:

- crayons or markers
- scissors
- oaktag
- glue
- clear contact paper
- Velcro

Glue

Directions:

1. Reproduce the rabbit and hat art on pages 13–14 ten times. Color the figures, mount them on oaktag, and cut them out.
2. On each rabbit, draw a clock face. Draw in hands showing a different time on each rabbit. On each hat, write out a time that matches the time shown on one of the rabbits.
3. Cover the rabbits and hats with clear contact paper.
4. Within the dotted circle on each hat, attach a piece of hard-backed Velcro. On the back of each rabbit, near the bottom, attach a piece of soft-backed Velcro.

4:30

5. Demonstrate to students how the rabbits may be placed on the hats. To use the activity, tell students that they should read the time on the clock shown on each hat and then find the rabbit with the matching clock.
6. When a match is found, the rabbit may be attached to the hat. When all the rabbits are in hats, have volunteers place the hats in correct time order, beginning with 12:00.
7. For additional challenge, write out a time equation on the hats, such as 1:45 + 20 minutes. Then draw a clock face on each rabbit, illustrating the answer to each time equation. Rabbits are then paired with hats by matching the time on their clocks with the correct equations.

12:00

1:00

3:00

The Magician's Hat

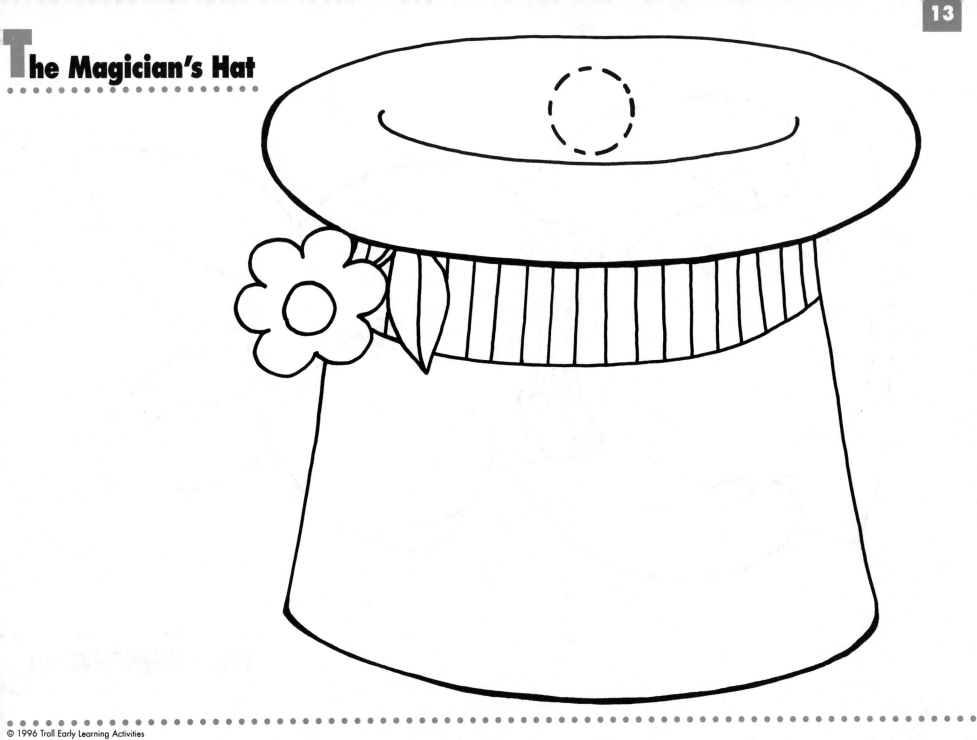

The Magician's Hat

Night and Day Interactive Poster

Materials:

- crayons or markers
- scissors
- oaktag
- clear contact paper
- Velcro
- sandwich-sized plastic bag
- glue

Directions:

1. Reproduce the art on pages 16–17 once. Color the figures, mount them on oaktag, and cut them out.

2. Cover the poster pieces with clear contact paper. On the back of each piece, attach a piece of soft-backed Velcro.

3. Draw a line down the middle of a large sheet of oaktag. Ask for two or three volunteers to color one half blue and the other half black. Ask a student to write "Day" on the blue side and another student to write "Night" on the black side. If students wish, they may add features that are characteristic of each half, such as a moon or sun.

4. On each half of the poster, randomly attach several pieces of hard-backed Velcro.

5. Explain to students that to play, they should take a picture from the bag, decide whether it is something that happens during the day or at night, then attach it to the correct side of the poster. Explain to the class that some pictures may be matched to either side. (For example, some people bathe in the morning, and others bathe at night.)

6. The poster may be used to distinguish between many things representative of night or day. For example, animals that are active during the night may be placed on the night side and animals that are active during the day may be placed on the day side. Events that occur during the day, such as eating lunch or going to school, may be used also. Objects that appear in the sky only at certain times are also a good source of day and night symbols: stars, moon, shooting stars, sun, rainbow.

7. Extra art may either be drawn or cut out from old magazines and workbooks. Mount the extra art on oaktag and cover it with clear contact paper. Place a piece of Velcro on the backs of these cards as well.

8. Store the poster cards in a plastic bag stapled to the bottom of the poster so that students will have easy access to them.

Night and Day Interactive Poster

The Order of Things Game

Materials:

- crayons or markers
- scissors
- 9" x 12" piece of oaktag
- glue
- 9" x 12" picture from a magazine
- folder with pockets inside

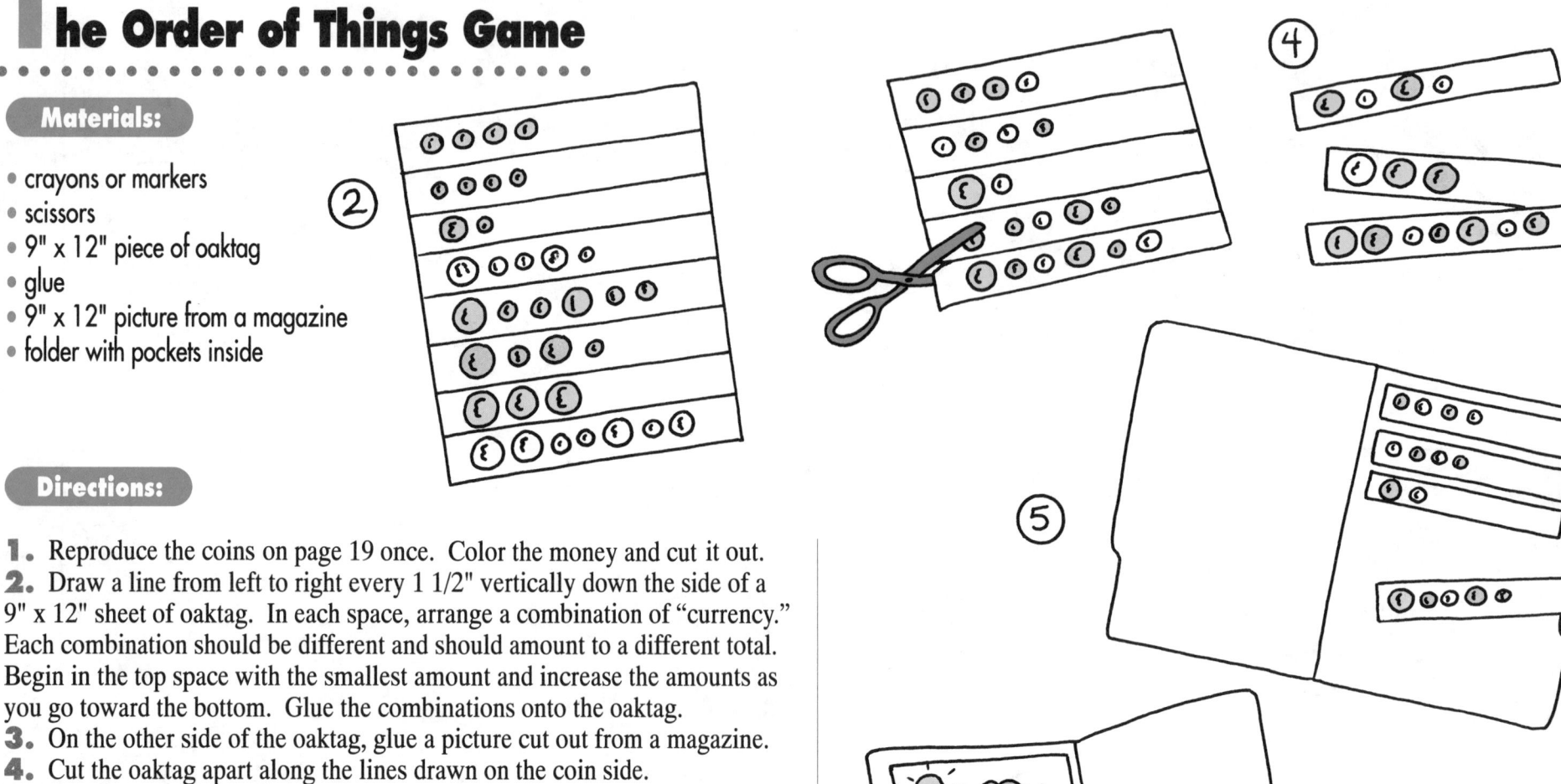

Directions:

1. Reproduce the coins on page 19 once. Color the money and cut it out.
2. Draw a line from left to right every 1 1/2" vertically down the side of a 9" x 12" sheet of oaktag. In each space, arrange a combination of "currency." Each combination should be different and should amount to a different total. Begin in the top space with the smallest amount and increase the amounts as you go toward the bottom. Glue the combinations onto the oaktag.
3. On the other side of the oaktag, glue a picture cut out from a magazine.
4. Cut the oaktag apart along the lines drawn on the coin side.
5. On the front of the folder, write the following directions: Open the folder and lay it flat. Add up the money shown on each strip. Place the strip showing the smallest amount at the top of the right side of the folder. Lay the strip showing the next smallest right under the first. Continue until the strip showing the largest amount is at the fold of the folder. Close the folder. Turn it over carefully so the back is facing front. Then open the folder. If the picture is pieced together correctly, the coin combinations are correct. If the picture is pieced together incorrectly, try again.
6. Place the strips inside the folder and place the folder in a math center for students' use during free time.

The Order of Things Game

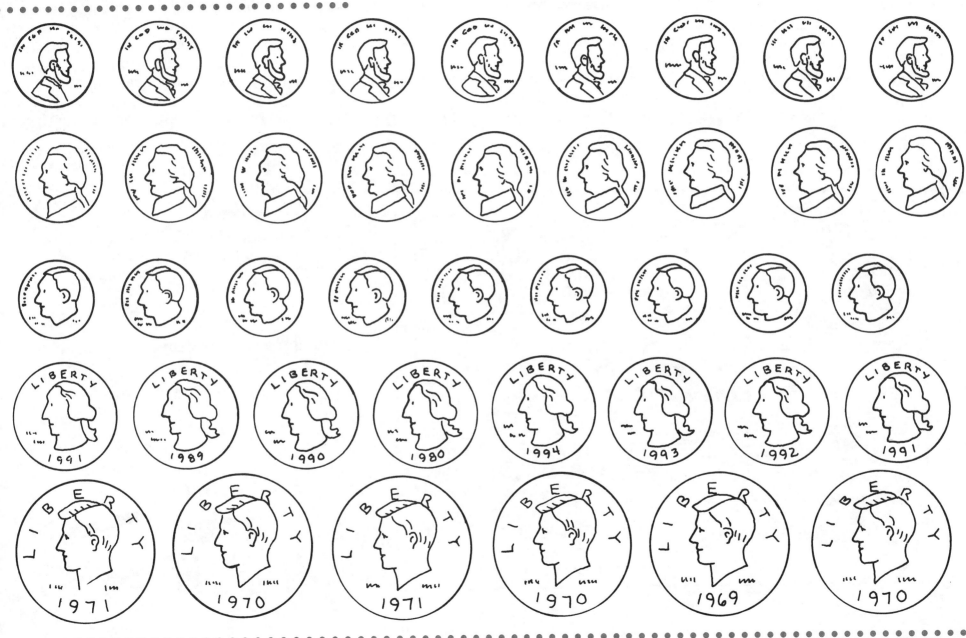

Piggy Bank Bulletin Board

Materials:

- crayons or markers
- scissors
- oaktag
- clear contact paper
- Velcro
- newspaper financial section
- stapler
- sandwich-sized plastic bag

FINANCE

$.55

$.40

$.85

$1.01

$1.50

$.91

Directions:

1. Reproduce the piggy bank art on page 21 ten times. Ask volunteers to color the piggy banks and cut them out.

2. Reproduce the coin art on page 19 several times. Ask volunteers to color the coins and cut them out.

3. On each bank, write a different money total. Then cover the banks and the coins with clear contact paper.

4. On the front of each bank, attach a strip of hard-backed Velcro. On the back of each coin, attach a piece of soft-backed Velcro.

5. Cover the bulletin board with the financial section of a newspaper. Staple the banks around the board, keeping them low enough for students to reach

them. Staple a clear, sandwich-sized plastic bag to the bottom of the board and place all the coins in it.

6. Explain to the class how to use the board. Choose a student to read the amount on a bank, select coins to equal that amount, and attach them to the bank. Choose another student to read the amount on the next bank and attach the correct coin combination. Continue with the other banks.

7. As each bank is filled, ask students if they can think of another combination of coins that would equal the amount on each bank. Encourage them to identify at least two ways of equaling each amount.

8. Store the coins in the plastic bag at the bottom of the bulletin board.

Piggy Bank Bulletin Board

Golfing for "Dollars"

Materials:

- five empty cans of the same size, tops left on
- different-colored construction paper
- tape
- markers
- golf balls
- golf club

Directions:

1. Cover each of five similarly sized cans (such as soup cans) with a different color of construction paper. Tape the paper securely around each can.

2. Lay the cans on the floor, spread out in a line, approximately 8" apart. On the top of each can, write a different dollar amount.

3. Demonstrate to the class how to play the game. Stand about two feet from the cans and place the golf ball on the floor in front of you. Grip the golf club and gently swing it as if to hit the ball in the direction of one of the cans. Explain that if the ball goes into the can, the player scores that amount. Amounts may be tallied on a piece of scrap paper or on the chalkboard. If the ball does not go into the can, the player must wait for his or her next turn to try again.

4. Inform the class that only three players may golf at a time. The youngest player goes first. Each player gets five turns. At the end of five turns, players may tally their scores. The winner is the player with the highest score.

Bobby	Brian	Becky
$2.00	$.25	$.0
$.60	$.60	

Money Worksheet

Make up a question for each math story below. Then trade questions with a classmate and try to figure out the answers to each other's questions.

1. Ted has a bushel of apples worth $3.60. A bushel holds 36 apples. Mary has $5.00. _____

2. Robby has 7 red candies, 5 yellow candies, and 9 blue candies. Each candy costs 5 cents. _____

3. Liam's House of Chocolates is having a sale. Every item in the store is half-price. He has items ranging from $1.00 to $25.00. _____

4. Admission prices to the concert depend on where you sit. The floor seats cost $30.00; balcony seats cost $25; and the upper-level seats cost $22.50. _____

5. Ben's back-to-school costs were as follows: pens—40 cents; pencils—60 cents; notebooks—$4.00; sharpener—30 cents; book covers—29 cents. _____

6. Frank works hard at his job. He makes $12.00 an hour. His sister Colleen makes $4.00 an hour. _____

Name _____

Dee's Discount Shop
· · · · · · · · · · · · · ·

Dee's Discount Shop is having a blowout sale! Figure out the final price for the discounted items below.

PANTS
$21.00
Take $10.00 off!

SHIRT
$16.00
Take $5.00 off!

1.

SNEAKERS
$29.00
Take $6.00 off!

2.

SOCKS
$6.50
for 3 pairs
Take $1.50 off!

HATS
$9.75 ea.
Take $3.00 off!

4.

BOOKBAG
$10.00
Take 50% off!

3.

5.

6.

Challenge: What would your total be if you purchased each of the items above? _____

Money Wheel

© 1996 Troll Early Learning Activities

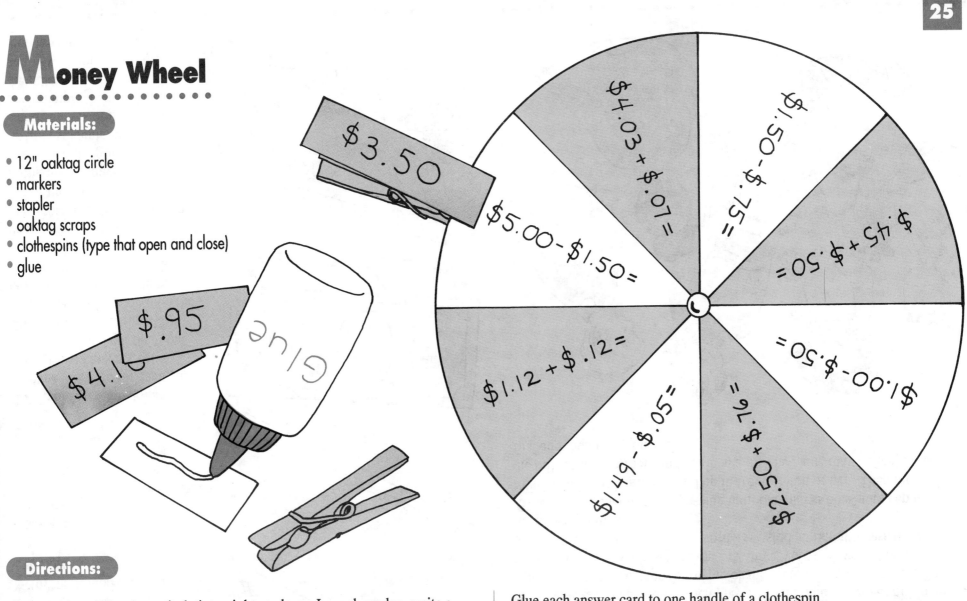

Materials:

- 12" oaktag circle
- markers
- stapler
- oaktag scraps
- clothespins (type that open and close)
- glue

Wheel equations:
- $4.03 + $.07 =
- $1.50 − $.75 =
- $.45 + $.50 =
- $1.00 − $.50 =
- $2.50 + $.76 =
- $1.49 − $.05 =
- $1.12 + $.12 =
- $5.00 − $1.50 =

Answer cards:
- $3.50
- $.95
- $4.10

Directions:

1. Divide a 12" oaktag circle into eight wedges. In each wedge, write a money equation geared toward the class's math level, such as "$2.50 + 76¢ =____."

2. Attach the circle to a bulletin board.

3. Cut oaktag scraps a little bigger than one of the handles on a clothespin. Write the answer to each of the money equations on an oaktag rectangle.

Glue each answer card to one handle of a clothespin.

4. Ask a student to read the equation in one of the wedges. Then have him or her find the clothespin with the correct answer on it and attach it to the wedge. Continue until students are familiar with the activity.

5. Create more money wheels to provide additional challenges for the class. Wheels may be stored in a large container on a shelf in the math center.

Pass the Buck

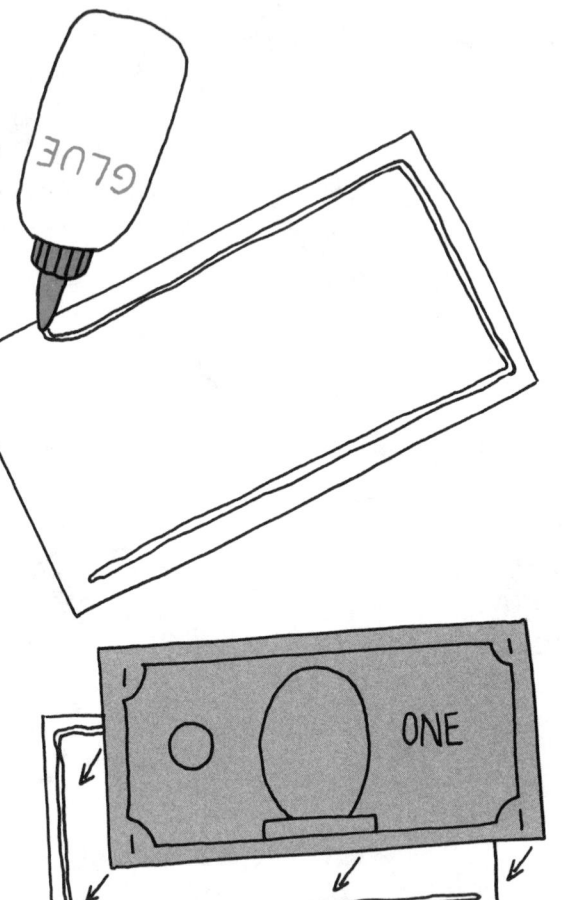

Materials:

- crayons or markers
- scissors
- glue
- newspaper
- transparent tape

Directions:

1. Reproduce the dollar art on page 27 twice for each student. Have students color their "bills" and cut them out.

2. Show students how to place one bill facedown on the table and squeeze a line of glue around three edges, leaving one short edge free. Then demonstrate how to carefully place the other bill faceup on top of the one on the table, lining up all edges.

3. When the glue is dry, instruct students to rip up small squares of newspaper and crumple them. Show them how to stuff their bills gently with the newspaper and then tape the open end closed.

4. Use the bills to play "Pass the Buck" with the class. Instruct students to sit cross-legged in a circle. Each player should hold his or her bill in one hand. Teach students the following chant: "Pass the buck, now . . . Pass the buck, now . . ." While saying the first three words, players should gently tap their bills on the floor. On the word *now*, students should pass their bills to the player on their right.

5. Continue chanting and passing until one player does not keep the rhythm and bills begin to build up in front of him or her. Then redistribute the bills to their owners and begin again. The game may be played slowly at first and then faster on each round.

Pass the Buck

Famous Faces

- glue
- scissors
- crayons or markers
- stapler
- oaktag

Directions:

1. Have a class discussion about the various famous faces that appear on bills and coins. (For example, George Washington is on the $1 bill, and Abraham Lincoln is on the penny.) Tell students that it is a great honor to be featured on money.

2. Ask each student to choose a famous person to research who is featured on a coin or bill. Provide the children with biographies, encyclopedias, and other research materials to use to write short reports telling why the person was chosen to be shown on a particular coin or bill.

3. Encourage students to share their reports with the rest of the class.

4. Reproduce the dollar bill pattern on page 27 once for each child. Have the children mount the bills on oaktag and cut them out.

5. Let students decorate the bills any way they choose. Tell the children that they should draw self-portraits in the center ovals of the bills.

6. Attach the student bills and reports on a bulletin board under the title, "Famous Faces Throughout History."

Name _____

Nursery Measurements

Solve the problems below. Show your work.

1. Mary had a little lamb whose fleece was white as snow. Mary's lamb weighs 17 pounds. If Mary has five other lambs, each weighing one pound more than the previous one, how much does her whole herd weigh? _____

2. The little dog laughed to see such a sight, and the dish ran away with the spoon. If the dish and the spoon can run 15 miles per hour, how far will they go in 3 hours? _____

3. The itsy, bitsy spider crawled up the water spout. The spider crawls up the spout ten times a day. If the spout is 10" long, how many inches will the spider crawl in a day? _____

4. Hickory, dickory, dock, the mouse ran up the clock. The mouse eats lunch at 1:00 P.M. every day and eats dinner 6 hours later. What time is the mouse's dinner? _____

5. Humpty Dumpty sat on a wall. Humpty Dumpty had a great fall. The king sent 12 men to put him together again. If each of the king's men had two pieces of Humpty Dumpty, how many pieces were there altogether? _____

Sorting Trees Bulletin Board

- crayons or markers
- scissors
- clear contact paper
- blue bulletin board paper
- brown construction paper
- Velcro
- gallon-sized clear plastic bag
- oaktag
- stapler

Directions:

1. Reproduce the leaf art on page 31 six times. Ask volunteers to color the leaves, mount them on oaktag, and cut them out.
2. Attach pieces of soft-backed Velcro to the backs of the leaves.
3. Cover a bulletin board with blue paper. Cut three trees with branches arranged randomly from brown construction paper—one small, one medium, and one large. Staple them in place with the base of their trunks at the base of the board.
4. On the tree branches, attach pieces of hard-backed Velcro, 36 in all. Draw in a sun, birds, clouds, and any other details desired.

5. Explain to the class how to use the board. Ask a student to pick up a leaf and tell the class what size it is: small, medium, or large. If the leaf is small, the student should stick it to the small tree. If the leaf is medium-sized, he or she should stick it to the medium-sized tree. And if the leaf is large, the student should stick it to the large tree.
6. Have students continue to attach the leaves to the trees according to size. When all the leaves have been used, ask a student to remove them and place them in a clear plastic bag. Ask the student to staple the bag to the bottom of the bulletin board. Encourage students to use the board during free time.

Sorting Trees Bulletin Board

Name _____

Nonstandard Estimations

Estimate the measurements of each item on the list below. Then use a ruler or tape measure to measure each item. Fill in the chart.

	Estimate	After Measuring
1. How tall are you?		
2. How long is the classroom? How wide?		
3. How wide is the teacher's desk?		
4. How tall is the door?		
5. How long is the hair of the person with the longest hair?		
6. How tall is your chair?		
7. How long would the line be if everyone in class put one shoe on the floor, touching toe to heel?		
8. How far is it to the school gym?		

Name _____

Oh, What a Tangled Web!

Estimate how long each web is, beginning at the center of each circle. Then take a piece of yarn and lay it over each web. Mark off the spot on the yarn where the web ends and measure it against a ruler.

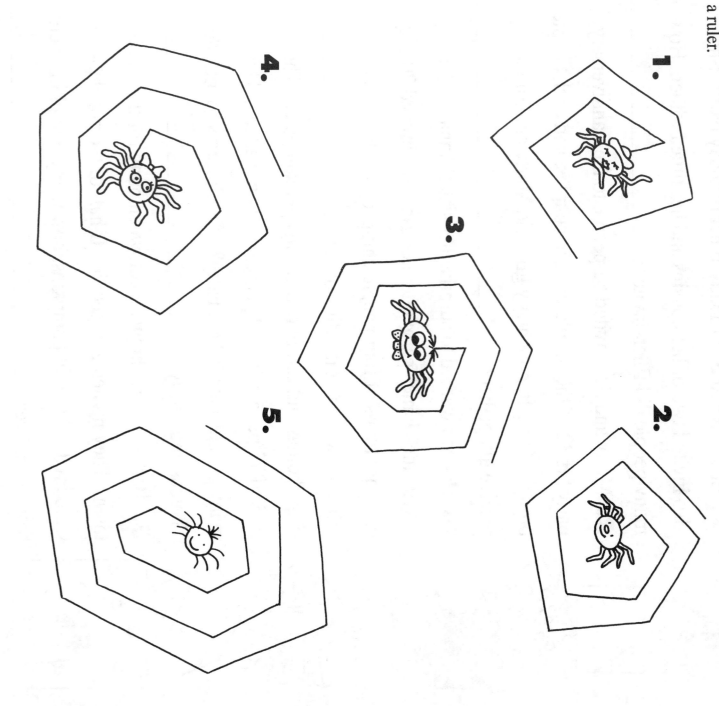

1.

2.

3.

4.

5.

Name _____

Party Time!

Figure out each of the party questions below.

1. Ellen invited five friends to her birthday party. She also invited two of her cousins and her little brother. How many people did Ellen invite? _____

2. Marty and Sue invited 62 people to their anniversary party. If 32 of the people were in couples, and each couple brought one gift, how many gifts did Marty and Sue receive altogether? _____

3. Hannah wanted to surprise her sister Anna with a "Welcome Home" party after her trip. She invited 20 people, but groups of four people chipped in to buy Anna's gifts. How many gifts did Anna receive? _____

4. Thomas and Emily had an engagement party. They invited 75 people, but 12 people could not attend. How many people attended the party? (Don't forget to include Thomas and Emily.) _____

5. Bart and Matt threw a Halloween party for the whole town. They invited 250 people. If half of the people who were invited brought pumpkins, how many pumpkins were there altogether? _____

Treasure Hunt

How many paces is it from "You are here" to the treasure? Use a piece of yarn to measure the path. Then measure the yarn against a ruler and look at the map scale to get your answer.

You are here

WARNING! QUICK SAND!

1 inch = 2 paces

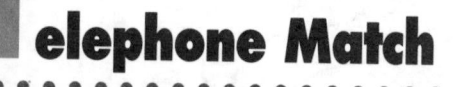elephone Match

Materials:

- crayons or markers
- scissors
- oaktag
- glue
- clear contact paper
- sticky-backed Velcro
- hole puncher
- yarn

Directions:

1. Reproduce the telephone art on page 37 ten times. Ask volunteers to color the art and cut it out. Leave the dials blank.

2. Mount the telephone bases, receivers, and dials on oaktag and cut them out again. Cover the telephone bases and receivers with clear contact paper.

3. Attach a piece of hard-backed Velcro to the center of each telephone base.

4. On each dial, write a length in inches or centimeters. Attach a piece of soft-backed Velcro to the back of each dial.

5. Punch a hole in the base of each receiver and the right side of each telephone base. Thread a length of yarn through the hole in each base and tie it. Tie the other end to a receiver. Make sure each of the resulting lengths equal one of the lengths written on a telephone dial.

6. Have a student measure the "cord" length of a telephone and then attach the matching dial to the phone base. When all the cords have been measured and the dials attached, have the student line the phones up in order from smallest to largest.

7. When a child has finished the activity, encourage the child to call a friend over to check his or her work.

Telephone Match

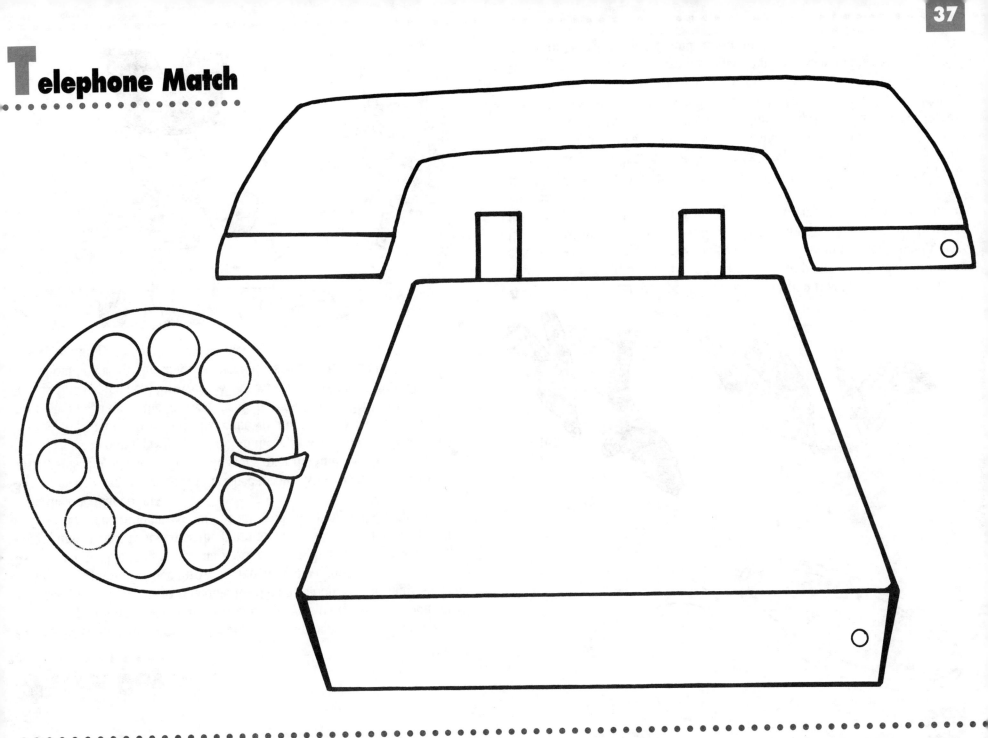

Sports Day

1. Hold a sports afternoon for the class. Ask students to brainstorm about sports competitions in which measurement plays a part. Discuss their ideas and decide which events to schedule for the afternoon. Some suggested events: long jump, Frisbee throw, kick ball, and weights.

2. To plan for the long jump, mark off a starting line on the playground. Mark a line at each foot across the jumping area. Write the measurement next to each line. Students should be allowed two jumps, the longer one being the one that counts.

3. Set aside a large area for the Frisbee throw. Mark a starting line where participants should stand. If a child steps over the line, the throw is disqualified. Ask two volunteers to stand out in the area where the Frisbees will be thrown. When a Frisbee lands, have the volunteers draw a circle around it and write the name of the thrower inside it, then run the Frisbee back to the starting line for the next thrower. When everyone has had a turn, the volunteers should measure the space between the starting line and the center of the Frisbee markings to determine a winner.

4. For the kick ball competition, mark a starting line for the participants. Place a large playground ball on the line. Participants should take a running start and kick the ball as far as they can. Volunteers in the field should mark the spots where the balls stop rolling. They may measure the space between the starting line and the places marked or use their judgment to determine the winner.

5. Fill plastic 1-liter bottles with sand. To participate in this activity, players will lift the bottles, completing as many repetitions as possible. Lifting should be done with a straight back and using only the arms. A lift is one in which a participant holds the weights at hip level, lifts them to his or her ears, then up in the air, and then slowly back to the ears and hips. The student who completes the most repetitions is the winner.

6. Try to include some activities that do not stress winning. Awards may be given for "terrific attitude" and "all-around player."

Sports Day

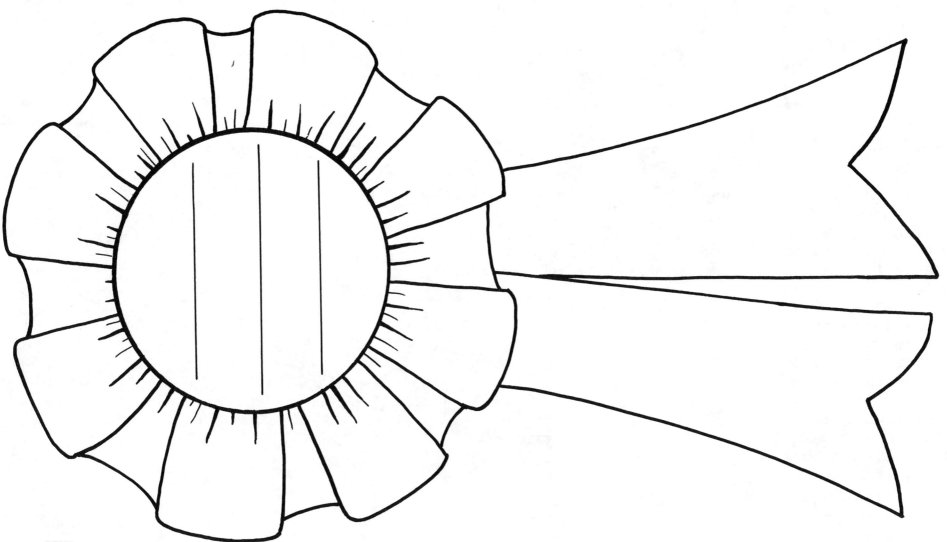

Fraction Bingo

Materials:

- crayons or markers
- glue
- oaktag
- scissors
- brass fastener
- colored pieces of oaktag
- envelope
- pocket folder

Directions:

1. Reproduce the game boards on pages 41–42 and the spinner on page 43 once each. Color the game boards, mount them on oaktag, and cut them out.
2. Color the spinner, mount it on oaktag, and cut it out. Use a brass fastener to attach the arrow to the spinner board so that the arrow moves freely.
3. Cut small squares from colored pieces of oaktag to cover the squares on the game board. Place the squares in an envelope.
4. Store the game boards, the spinner, and the envelope inside a pocket folder.

How to Play
(for two players)
1. Each player takes a game board. Players should place the envelope with the colored squares between them.
2. Players take turns spinning. After a spin, the player announces the fraction that is shown on the spinner (e.g., "1/4," "1/2", "1/5").
3. Each player looks at his or her game board to see if the fraction appears. If the fraction does appear, the player covers it with a colored square. If a fraction appears more than once, the player may choose which of the squares to cover on that turn.
4. Play continues until one player completes the agreed-upon configuration for bingo, such as a single row or column, an X, a T, a "picture frame," or covering the entire board.

Fraction Bingo

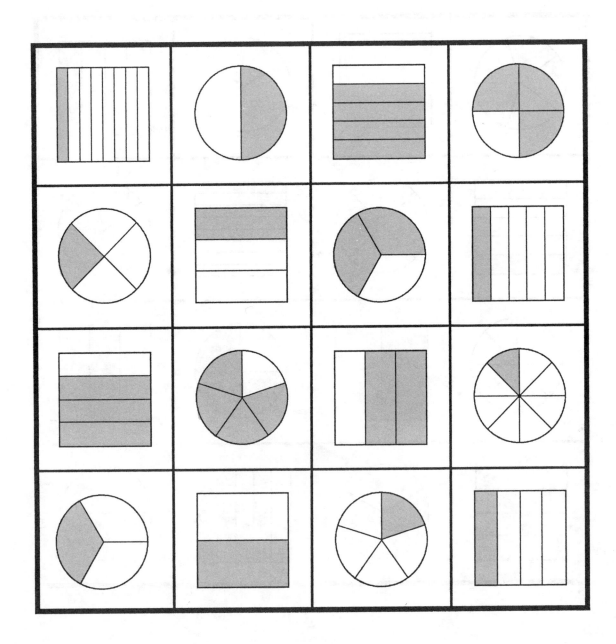

Fraction Bingo

Fraction Bingo

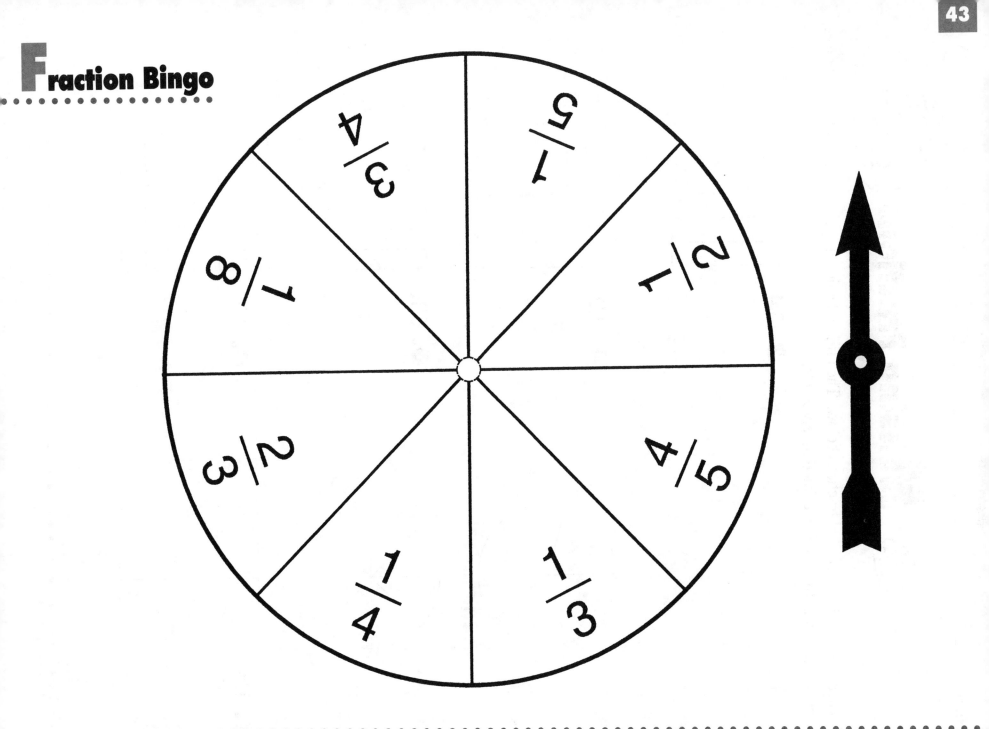

Name _____

Missing Fractions

Look at each of the numbered fractions below. Then fill in the drawing to the right of the fraction to show the part of the whole the fraction represents.

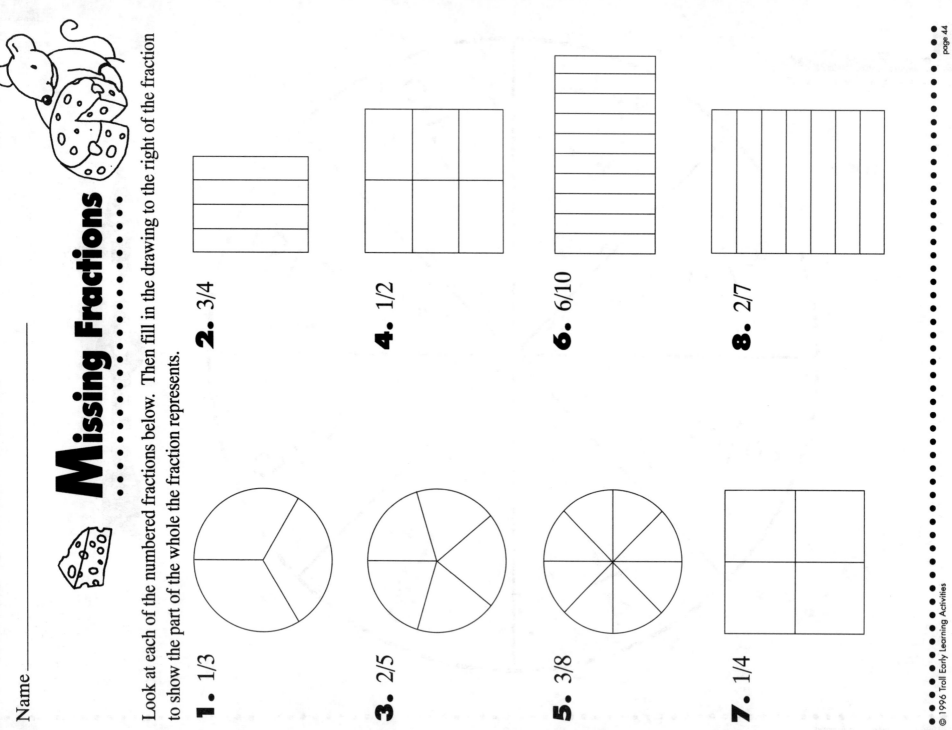

1. 1/3

2. 3/4

3. 2/5

4. 1/2

5. 3/8

6. 6/10

7. 1/4

8. 2/7

Fun With Fractions

Look at each of the numbered drawings below. On the line provided, write the fraction that is shown by the shaded portion of the drawing.

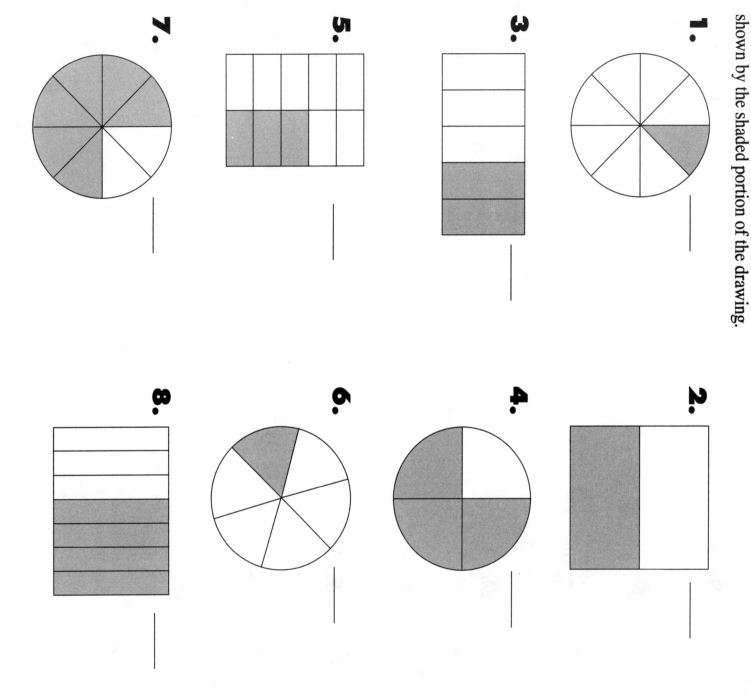

1. _____

2. _____

3. _____

4. _____

5. _____

6. _____

7. _____

8. _____

Name _____

Roman **Numerals**

Match each numeral on the left with its Roman numeral.

A. 6

B. 10

C. 8

D. 7

E. 1

F. 5

G. 3

H. 4

I. 9

J. 2

VII

IX

VI

II

IV

X

III

VIII

I

V

Name _____

Roman Holiday

Julius is on vacation and wants to do some shopping. One of the stores he visits has all of its price tags written in Roman numerals. Help Julius figure out how much each of the items below costs. On the lines provided, write the price in standard numerals for each Roman numeral price.

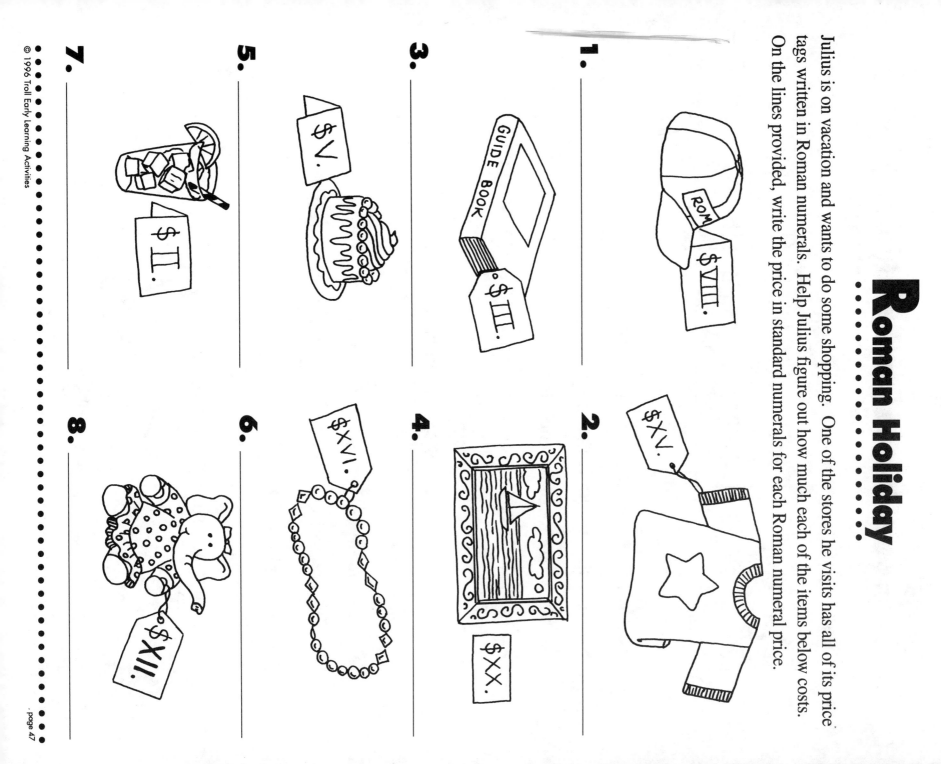

1. ROMA $VIII.

2. $XV.

3. GUIDE BOOK $III.

4. $XX.

5. $V. $II.

6. $XVI.

7. _____

8. $XII.

Counting in Roman Numerals

Answer the questions below, using Roman numerals.

1. How old are you? _____

2. How many students are in your class? _____

3. How many people are in your family? _____

4. On what day of the month were you born? _____

5. How many steps is it from your bedroom to the kitchen in your home? _____

6. How many hours of television have you watched in the past week? _____

7. How many players are there on a baseball team? _____   On a soccer team? _____

On a basketball team? _____

8. What grade are you in? _____

9. How many days are there in this month? _____

10. How many sides does an octagon have? _____

Farm Chores File-Folder Game

Materials:

- crayons or markers
- scissors
- glue
- letter-sized file folder
- clear contact paper (optional)
- envelope
- clay
- die
- pennies, nickels, and dimes

Directions:

1. Reproduce the game board on pages 50–51 once. Color the game board, cut it out, and mount it on the inside of a letter-sized file folder.

2. Reproduce the game cards on page 52 four times. Color the cards, mount them on oaktag, and cut them out. Laminate if desired.

3. Use pennies, nickels, and dimes for playing pieces. Make each playing piece a base from a small ball of clay so that it will stand up.

4. Glue an envelope to the back of the file folder. Store the game cards in the envelope, along with the playing pieces and a die.

How to Play
(for two to four players)

1. Each player places his or her playing piece at "Start." Place the game cards in a pile next to the game board.

2. Each player rolls the die once. The player with the highest number goes first. Play continues clockwise around the game board.

3. The first player rolls the die and moves the indicated number of spaces around the game board. If the player lands on a "chore" space, he or she may draw a card from the pile.

4. Play continues. The first player to "Finish" his or her chores receives a bonus of $.25. All players then tally their chore cards. The player who has earned the most money is the winner.

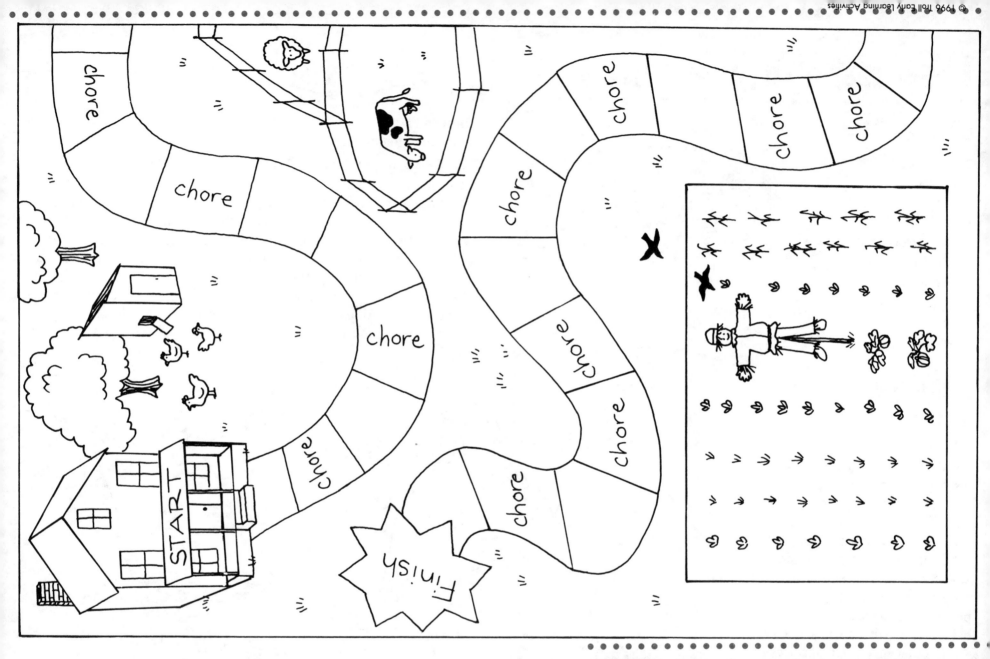

Farm Chores File-Folder Game

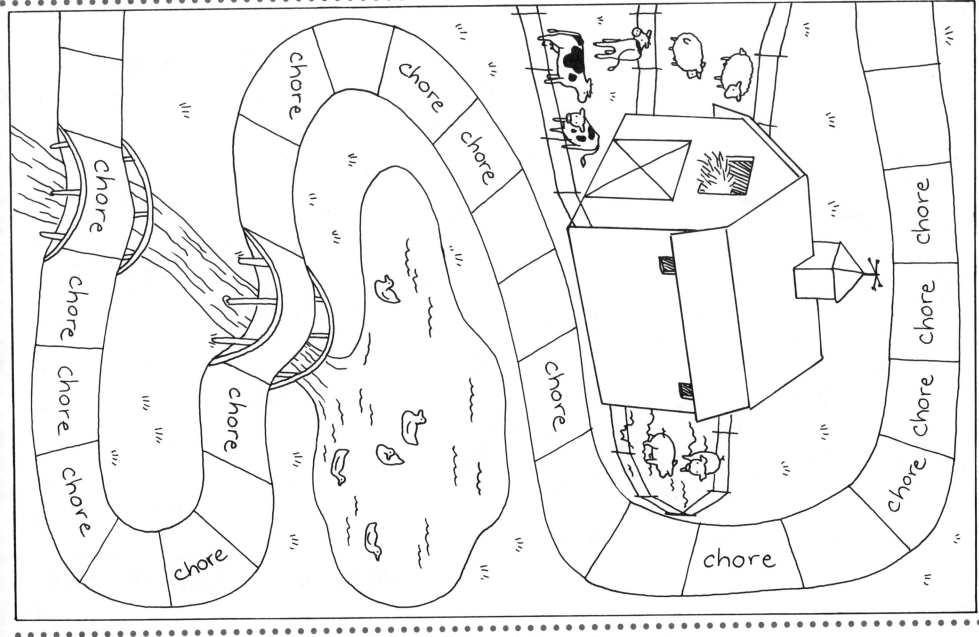

Farm Chores File-Folder Game

Milk cows. $1.00	Milk cows. $1.00	Bale hay. $.75	Feed pigs. $1.25	Weed garden. $1.50
Gather eggs. $.75	Gather eggs. $.75	Take a rest. Lose a turn!	Put sheep in pen. $1.00	Clean stalls. $1.50
Plant seeds. $.50	Put goats in pen. $1.00	Make scarecrow. $1.00	Water garden. $.50	Feed ducks. $1.25

Sarah's Secret Plan

Read the following story about a girl whose parents are always running late.

Sarah's Secret Plan
Written by Linda Johns
Illustrated by Denise Brunkus

Sarah was waiting. Impatiently waiting.

She hoped her father would see that she was serious about getting to Ms. Wickstone's class on time.

"I'm running a little late, Sarah," her father called from upstairs. She could hear him hopping across the bedroom on one foot, trying to put a shoe on the other foot while he brushed his teeth. What he said actually sounded like "Aim gunning uh widdle ate, Ah-rah."

Sarah, of course, knew exactly how he was hopping and what he was saying. It was the same every Wednesday.

On Mondays, Tuesdays, Thursdays, and Fridays, Sarah took the bus to Amelia Earhart Elementary School. She loved taking the bus. On bus days, Sarah was always on time for school.

Wednesdays were a different story. On Wednesdays Sarah's dad dropped her off at school on his way to a weekly meeting.

"I would never miss taking my favorite daughter to school on Wednesdays," Sarah's dad always said with a chuckle.

This was her father's idea of a joke. You see, Sarah was his only daughter. In fact, she was his only child.

Sarah's mom was always late, too. "Gotta go, or I'll be late for work," Sarah's mom said each morning as she ran out the door.

Sarah's parents were late for everything. Even on weekends. Even for fun things, like going to the movies.

"The movie's just started," the ticket taker would say as Sarah and her parents rushed through the theater door.

"No time for popcorn," Sarah's dad would call as they hurried through the lobby and into the dark theater.

"Excuse me. Oh, so sorry!" Sarah's mom would say as they climbed over people to get to their seats.

Of course, the only seats left were always right behind tall grown-ups.

Sarah sighed as she thought about all the times she'd been late to movies. But right now it was Wednesday morning, and she wished her father would hurry up and get her to school.

That night, Sarah thought up the most incredible plan in the history of kids. Sarah's Secret Plan would make Wednesdays run on time.

She waited until Tuesday night. Then Sarah put the Secret Plan into motion.

First she sneaked into her parents' bedroom. Then she crept into the bathroom and back downstairs to the kitchen.

Sarah's Secret Plan

Finally, she took care of the living room while her mother was on the phone.

Sarah checked each item off her Secret Plan list.

> ✓ 2 alarm clocks
> ✓ 1 clock radio
> ✓ red wall clock
> ✓ Dad's watch (nightstand)
> ✓ Mom's watch (dresser)
> ✓ oven clock
> ✓ microwave clock
> ✓ living room clock

And for the final, most convincing part of the Secret Plan, Sarah set the clock on the VCR, which for some reason always flashed "12:00."

The next day was Wednesday. Sarah's father hopped around and called down to her, "Aim gunning uh widdle ate, Ah-rah."

But Sarah wasn't worried this time. She knew her dad only thought he was late. He was actually on time, thanks to the Secret Plan.

Sarah was on time for school that Wednesday. That weekend, Sarah's family made it to a movie before it started. In fact, they were early enough to get popcorn and Sarah's favorite flavor of Wild 'n' Wacky Fruit Chews.

The Secret Plan had worked! All the clocks and watches in Sarah's house were set ten minutes ahead. And now her family was always on time.

Sarah was blissfully happy—and on time—for several days. Then things started going wrong.

"Sarah, it's time to get ready for bed," her mother said on Sunday night.

"But there are almost ten minutes left in *The Burples*," Sarah said. *The Burples* was Sarah's favorite television show.

"My watch says it's eight o'clock, and that means it's time for bed," Sarah's mother said.

The Secret Plan Code of Super Secrecy meant Sarah couldn't tell her mother what time it really was.

On Monday night Sarah's father was in the middle of a bedtime story when he glanced at his watch. "Oops. That's it for tonight," he said as he put the book away.

Sarah didn't say anything, even though she really would have liked to have heard the end of the story.

On Tuesday morning Sarah's father said, "Sarah, you'd better get out to the corner and wait for the bus now."

It was pouring rain. And the bus wouldn't arrive for another ten minutes. But Sarah couldn't say anything without revealing her Secret Plan.

That afternoon Sarah was playing with her friends Sophie and Nicole when her mother came to pick her up ten whole minutes early. "Time to go, Sarah," Sarah's mom said.

"But Mom . . ." said Sarah.

"Yes?" replied Sarah's mother. She looked at Sarah with her eyebrows raised.

Sarah sighed. "Nothing. See you tomorrow, guys."

Sarah knew she had to do something. If she didn't act

Sarah's Secret Plan

fast, she might never again see the end of *The Burples*, or hear a complete bedtime story, or finish playing a game with her friends.

It was time for Secret Plan Number 2.

That evening Sarah sneaked back into action. She worked on the clocks in the bedroom, the kitchen, the bathroom, and the living room. She even worked on her parents' watches. She set all the clocks back ten minutes. Now all the clocks in Sarah's house were set for the right time.

Sarah went to bed right on time—the right time—that night. But then she awoke with a start in the middle of the night. She'd forgotten to set the clock on the VCR!

Sarah rushed downstairs to the family room. And that's where she found the note.

Dear Sarah,
Now that you've gotten us to be on time, we've found that we actually like it. From now on, we promise to be on time—especially on Wednesdays.
Love,
Mom and Dad

Time Charts

When We Start Our School Day					
Name	Mon.	Tues.	Wed.	Thurs.	Fri.
Rachel	9:02	9:00			
Max	9:00	8:45			
Rob	X	9:00			
Susan	9:01	8:59			
Lisa	9:00	8:56			
José	8:56	8:59			
Mary	8:57	9:00			
John	9:02	9:00			

1. After reading "Sarah's Secret Plan" with the class, discuss the concepts of "early" and "late." Ask if anyone has a family like Sarah's, whose members are usually running late. Ask if still other students have families whose members are usually on time. Which do students prefer?

2. Use a large piece of oaktag to make a chart with each student's name in a column along the left side. Draw in a grid showing a certain number of days (e.g., a week, two weeks, or a month) next to the column of names, as shown.

3. Tell students that they will be "punching in" each morning when they arrive in the classroom. When a child arrives, have him or her record the exact time in the appropriate box on the grid. Draw in an *X* for any child who is absent on a particular day.

4. At the end of the designated period of time, ask students to examine the chart carefully. Have each child tell the time at which he or she most frequently arrived, the latest time of arrival, and the earliest time of arrival.

5. Make a class graph that shows the various times of arrival. Title the chart and the graph, "When We Start Our School Day."

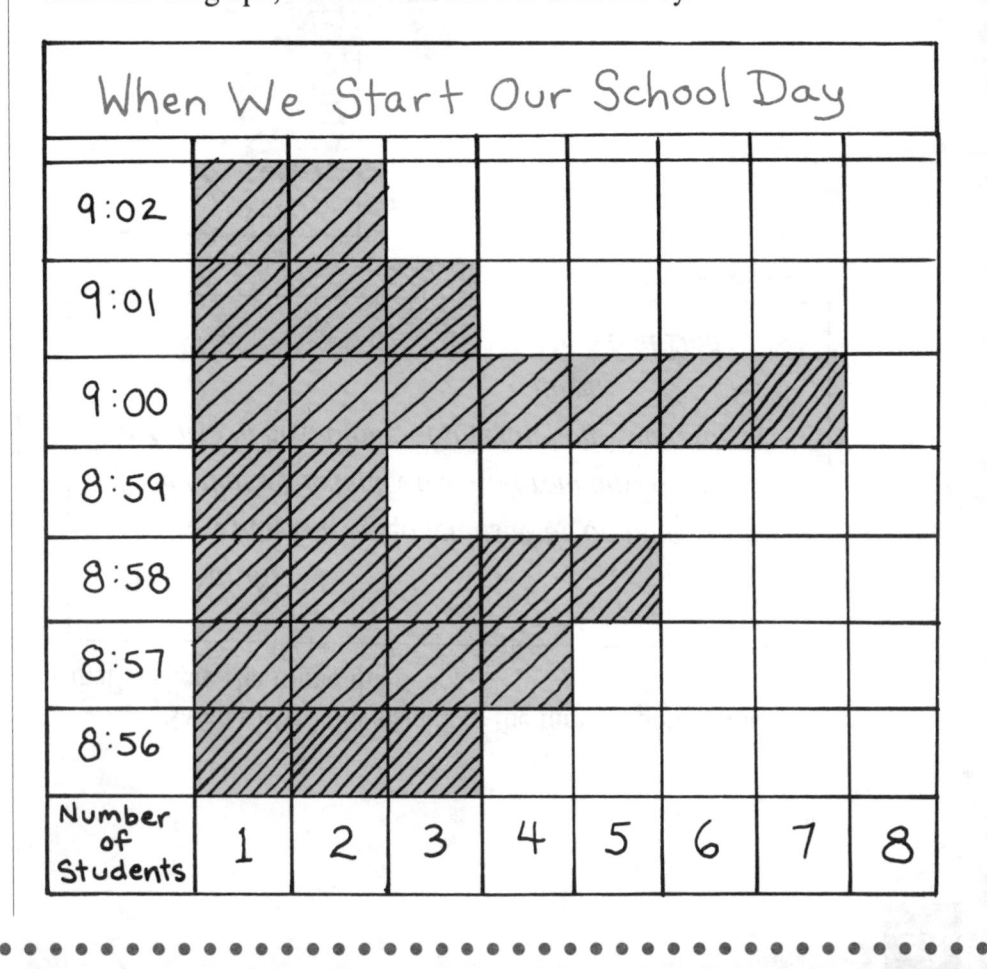

Name _____

Sarah's Story

After listening to the story "Sarah's Secret Plan," answer the questions below.

1. Why was Sarah always late for school on Wednesdays? _____

2. Why did Sarah want to get to the movies earlier? _____

3. How much ahead did Sarah set the clocks in her house? _____

4. What happened when Sarah was watching *The Burples*? _____

5. Why did Sarah decide to change the clocks back to the correct time? _____

6. How do you think Sarah's parents found out about her Secret Plan? _____

Name _____

Sarah's Schedule
. . . .

Read the sentences below. For each group of sentences, tell if Sarah was early, late, or on time.

1. School started at 9:00 .

Sarah got to school at 8:55 .

Sarah was _____ .

2. The movie started at 2:15 .

Sarah got to her seat at 2:30 .

Sarah was _____ .

3. The bus arrived at 8:25 .

Sarah got to the bus stop at 8:15 .

Sarah was _____ .

4. The birthday party started at 3:30 .

Sarah arrived at 3:30 .

Sarah was _____ .

5. Sarah had a doctor's appointment at 11:45 .

Sarah got to the doctor's office at 11:40 .

Sarah was _____ .

Name _____

My Weekly Schedule

Use the weekly schedule below to plan your activities for each week. You may wish to write down your homework times, special meeting or activity times, or other important appointments.

Book report due

Give Skippy a bath

Sleep over at Gary's

	Mon	Tues	Wed	Thurs	Fri	Sat/Sun

Birthday party

$\begin{array}{r} 10 \\ +7 \\ \hline 17 \end{array}$ Math

math homework

Softball practice

Timed Test

Name _____

See how many of these addition problems you can complete in three minutes. Try again each day to see if your score improves!

7 + 3 = 10	5 + 2 =	3 + 6 =	1 + 9 =
2 + 5 =	6 + 2 =	8 + 2 =	7 + 1 =
5 + 3 =	9 + 0 =	6 + 4 =	4 + 2 =
8 + 2 =	3 + 1 =	9 + 0 =	3 + 1 =
3 + 6 =	3 + 3 =	5 + 5 =	0 + 1 =
4 + 3 =	5 + 1 = 6	8 + 1 =	1 + 9 =
9 + 1 =	4 + 6 =	7 + 2 =	1 + 4 =
10 + 0 =	4 + 1 =	7 + 3 =	4 + 3 =
5 + 5 =	7 + 0 =	1 + 8 =	2 + 6 =
7 + 1 =	4 + 4 =	1 + 9 =	2 + 8 =
1 + 6 =	4 + 0 =	5 + 3 =	6 + 4 =
2 + 1 =	1 + 1 =	2 + 2 =	3 + 7 =
4 + 4 =	2 + 2 =	3 + 3 =	8 + 2 =
0 + 9 =	0 + 0 =	1 + 6 =	9 + 1 =
8 + 1 =	3 + 1 =	1 + 5 =	6 + 0 =
1 + 9 =	1 + 6 =	1 + 4 =	4 + 3 =
8 + 0 =	5 + 3 =	1 + 3 =	3 + 5 =
6 + 4 =	7 + 2 =	0 + 5 =	3 + 2 =
9 + 1 =	5 + 4 =	5 + 1 =	2 + 3 =
7 + 1 =	4 + 5 =	3 + 5 =	5 + 4 =
6 + 3 =	4 + 4 =	3 + 6 =	6 + 2 =
2 + 7 =	0 + 3 =	2 + 2 =	7 + 3 =
2 + 8 =	5 + 2 =	3 + 4 =	2 + 1 =
3 + 2 =	2 + 6 =	5 + 2 = 7	5 + 5 =
4 + 2 =	3 + 4 =	2 + 6 =	4 + 6 =

Name _____

Timed Test

See how many of these subtraction problems you can complete in three minutes. Try again each day to see if your score improves!

7 - 3 =	5 - 2 =	8 - 7 =	7 - 6 =
9 - 6 =	6 - 2 =	8 - 2 =	7 - 1 =
5 - 3 =	9 - 8 =	9 - 3 =	4 - 2 =
8 - 2 =	3 - 1 =	9 - 2 =	3 - 1 =
8 - 5 =	3 - 3 =	5 - 5 =	8 - 7 =
4 - 3 =	5 - 1 =	8 - 3 =	9 - 8 =
9 - 1 =	6 - 4 =	7 - 2 =	9 - 4 =
10 - 0 =	4 - 1 =	7 - 3 =	4 - 3 =
5 - 5 =	7 - 0 =	8 - 4 =	8 - 6 =
7 - 1 =	4 - 4 =	8 - 5 =	7 - 5 =
7 - 6 =	1 - 1 =	5 - 3 =	6 - 4 =
2 - 1 =	4 - 0 =	2 - 2 =	8 - 6 =
4 - 4 =	2 - 2 =	3 - 3 =	9 - 5 =
9 - 7 =	0 - 0 =	9 - 6 =	9 - 1 =
8 - 1 =	3 - 1 =	8 - 3 =	6 - 0 =
9 - 1 =	6 - 1 =	9 - 5 =	4 - 3 =
8 - 0 =	5 - 3 =	7 - 6 =	6 - 5 =
6 - 4 =	7 - 2 =	8 - 4 =	7 - 6 =
7 - 1 =	5 - 4 =	7 - 4 =	5 - 4 =
6 - 3 =	8 - 4 =	7 - 3 =	6 - 2 =
7 - 5 =	9 - 4 =	7 - 3 =	7 - 3 =
9 - 3 =	9 - 2 =	8 - 5 =	2 - 1 =
3 - 2 =	7 - 4 =	9 - 7 =	5 - 5 =
4 - 2 =	7 - 6 =	8 - 3 =	7 - 3 =

Time Award

Presented to

_____

for terrific time-telling skills.

_____

_____

ath Award

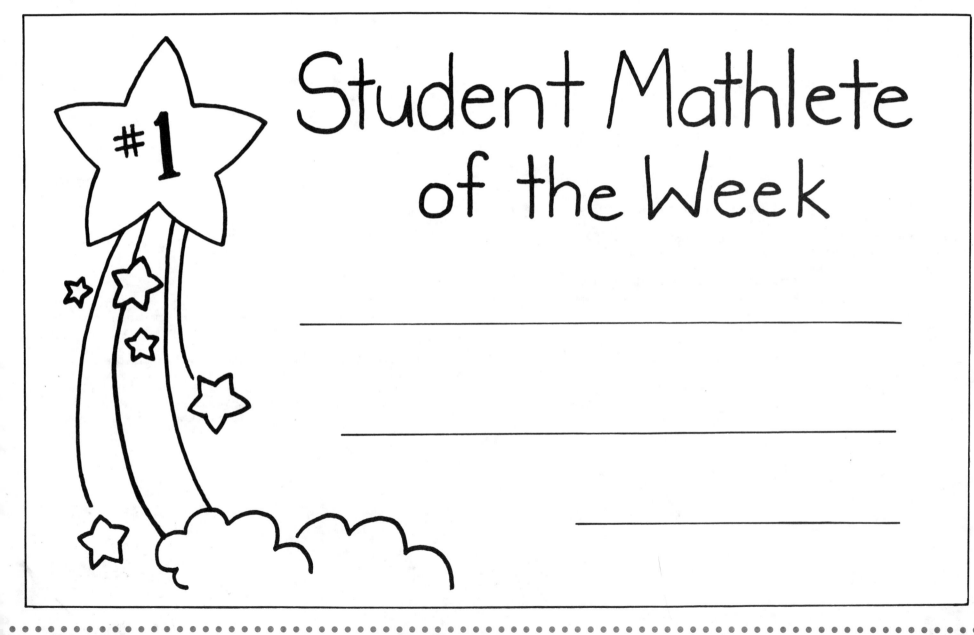

Student Mathlete
of the Week

Answers

page 9

1. Neither was fastest—their times were the same
2. Claudia
3. 3
4. the baby who was six months old
5. 15 years old

page 11

Answers will vary.

page 23

Answers will vary. Possible answers include:
1. Mary wants to buy 18 apples. How much will they cost? ($1.80)
2. How many candies does Robbie have altogether? (21) How much did the candies cost? ($1.05)
3. If a one-pound box of chocolates is usually $12.50, how much would the sale price be? ($6.25)
4. You are taking three of your friends to the concert. You have $100.00. Which tickets can you buy? (4 balcony seats)
5. Ben gave the cashier a $10.00 bill. How much change did he get back? ($4.41)
6. Frank and Colleen each worked eight hours today. How much did each of them make? (Frank: $96.00; Colleen: $32.00)

page 24

1. $11.00
2. $11.00
3. $5.00
4. $23.00
5. $5.00
6. $6.75
Challenge: $61.75

page 29

1. 117 pounds
2. 45 miles
3. 200 (remember—he has to crawl down, too!)
4. 7:00 P.M.
5. 24

page 32

Answers will vary.

page 33

1. 9"
2. 11 1/2"
3. 13 1/4"
4. 15"
5. 20"

page 34

1. 8
2. 46
3. 5
4. 65
5. 125

page 35

48 (24 inches)

page 44

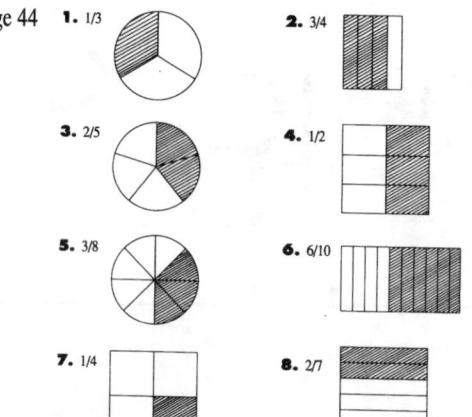

1. 1/3
2. 3/4
3. 2/5
4. 1/2
5. 3/8
6. 6/10
7. 1/4
8. 2/7

page 45

1. 1/8
2. 1/2
3. 2/5
4. 3/4
5. 3/10
6. 1/6
7. 6/8
8. 4/7

page 47

1. $8.00
2. $15.00
3. $3.00
4. $20.00
5. $5.00
6. $16.00
7. $2.00
8. $12.00

page 48

Answers will vary.

page 46

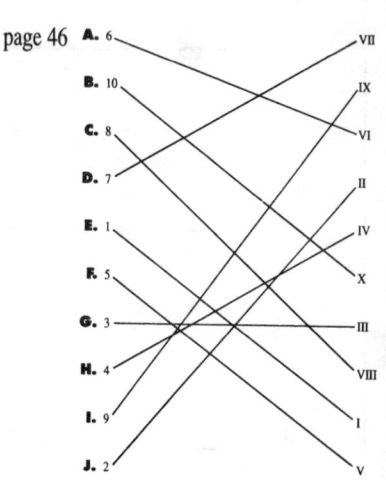

A. 6   B. 10   C. 8   D. 7   E. 1   F. 5   G. 3   H. 4   I. 9   J. 2

VII, IX, VI, II, IV, X, III, VIII, I, V

page 57

1. Instead of taking the bus, she was driven to school by her father.
2. Because she and her parents never had time to get popcorn.
3. ten minutes
4. Sarah's mom looked at the clock and told Sarah it was time for bed, but the TV show wasn't over.
5. She kept missing out on play time, stories, and TV-show endings because the clocks were set ahead ten minutes.
6. Answers will vary. Possible answers include: "They noticed the VCR clock no longer flashed '12:00'."

page 58

1. early
2. late
3. early
4. on time
5. early